Countries of the World

Greece

by Janet Riehecky

Consultants:
Athanasios Apostolopoulos and Helen Sofos
Hellenic American Cultural Association of Colorado

Bridgestone Books
an imprint of Capstone Press
Mankato, Minnesota

Bridgestone Books are published by Capstone Press
151 Good Counsel Drive, P.O. Box 669, Mankato, Minnesota 56002
http://www.capstone-press.com

Library of Congress Cataloging-in-Publication Data
Riehecky, Janet, 1953–
   Greece/by Janet Riehecky.
   p. cm.—(Countries of the world)
   Includes bibliographical references and index.
   Summary: Discusses the land, history, people, food, clothes, sports, and culture of Greece.
   ISBN 0-7368-0628-8
   1. Greece—Civilization—Juvenile literature. [1. Greece.] I. Title. II. Countries of the world
(Mankato, Minn.)
DF741 .R54 2001
949.5—dc21   00-023723

Editorial Credits

Tom Adamson, editor; Timothy Halldin, designer; Heidi Schoof and Kimberly Danger,
      photo researchers

Photo Credits

Betty Crowell, 8
Bruce Coleman Inc./Guido Cozzi, 10
Index Stock Imagery, 16
Photri-Microstock, cover
Root Resources/Byron Crader, 6
StockHaus Limited, 5 (top)
Trip/H. Rogers, 5 (bottom); A. Tovy, 12; P. Richards, 20
Unicorn Stock Photos/Mary Morina, 14
Vladimir Pcholkin/FPG International LLC, 18

1 2 3 4 5 6 06 05 04 03 02 01

Table of Contents

Fast Facts

Official Name: Hellenic Republic
Capital: Athens
Population: More than 10.5 million
Language: Greek
Religion: Greek Orthodox

Size: 50,942 square miles
(131,940 square kilometers)
*Greece is a little smaller than the
U.S. state of New York.*
Crops: Cotton, grapes, olives

Maps

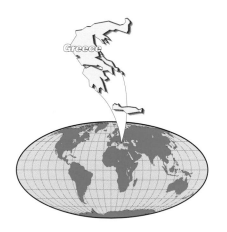

4

Flag

The Greek flag has nine stripes. Five blue stripes stand for the sky and the sea. Four white stripes stand for the purity of Greece's fight for freedom. A white cross is in the top left-hand corner. The cross stands for Greek Orthodox Christianity. This flag has been used since 1830. It became the official national flag in 1978.

Currency

The unit of currency in Greece is the drachma.

In 2000, about 367 drachmas equaled 1 U.S. dollar. About 247 drachmas equaled 1 Canadian dollar.

The Land

Greece is in southeastern Europe. Albania, the Former Yugoslav Republic of Macedonia, Bulgaria, and Turkey border northern Greece.

Most of Greece forms a peninsula. The Mediterranean, Ionian, and Aegean Seas surround the country. No place in Greece is more than 85 miles (137 kilometers) from the sea. Thousands of islands also are part of Greece. Crete is the largest Greek island.

Mountains and plains cover most of Greece. Mountains cover about three-fourths of the country. The tallest mountain is Mount Olympus. Ancient Greeks believed the gods lived there. Flat coastal plains cover less than 20 percent of Greece. Farmers grow crops on the plains.

Greece has about 9,000 miles (14,500 kilometers) of coastline. The coastline has many rocky bays and sandy beaches.

Seas cut into the land along the coast of Greece.

Ancient Greece

About 2,500 years ago, Greece enjoyed a Golden Age. During that time, the Greeks invented democracy, wrote famous stories, and made many beautiful buildings.

Towns in ancient Greece formed city-states. Each city-state had its own government. Men 18 and older were citizens. Citizens in each city-state voted to elect their leaders. Women and slaves could not vote in ancient Greece.

Ancient Greeks believed that many gods and goddesses controlled their lives. They worshipped these gods and goddesses and told stories about them.

Ancient Greeks built many beautiful buildings. Most buildings were temples honoring a god or a goddess. Many tourists visit the ruins of these buildings today. The most famous of these buildings is the Parthenon. This building was dedicated to the goddess Athena.

The Parthenon was built nearly 2,500 years ago.

Life at Home

Today, Greeks' lives are a lot like those of people in cities and towns in North America. Adults go to work. Children go to school. For fun, families go to sporting events, the theater, and museums.

City neighborhoods are friendly. People watch out for one another and treat strangers with kindness. In the evening, families often go for a walk. They stop to talk to people they meet.

Greeks are loyal to their families and take care of family members. Many homes include grandparents. Young married couples often live with the husband's parents.

In the past, the father was in charge of the family. Mothers usually stayed home. They took care of the children and the house. More women now have jobs outside the home. Many husbands and wives make decisions about the family together.

Many Greeks are friendly and like to talk.

Most Greek children attend public schools.

Going to School

Greek children must go to school between the ages of 6 and 15. Almost all children go to public schools. Children attend school Monday through Friday. Greek children study reading, math, history, and geography. In third grade, they start studying religion.

Greek children usually go to three different schools. They have six years of primary school. They then attend a gymnasium, or junior high, for three years. Most students continue for three more years at a lyceum (LEE-key-um), a senior high school.

Students must pass a test to go to a university. Some students take extra classes to help them do well on the test. Getting into a university is not easy. There are not enough places for all the students who want to attend a university.

Greek Food

Sharing food with family and guests is important to Greek people. Meals are social times. Greeks usually have coffee and a pastry for breakfast. The main meal of the day usually is between 2 p.m. and 3 p.m. In the evening, Greeks often have a late supper in a restaurant.

Greek cooks use only the freshest ingredients. They cook foods in olive oil and choose herbs and spices carefully. Seafood is popular and easy to find in local markets. Fish, octopus, and squid are favorites. Almost every meal includes a salad with olive oil.

One famous Greek food is the kebab. People put chunks of meat and vegetables on a skewer. They hold this long, thin metal spear over a fire to cook the food.

Baklava is a favorite dessert. This baked pastry is filled with honey and nuts.

Kebabs are chunks of food on a skewer.

Clothing

Most Greeks today wear the same kind of clothes that people in North America wear. But they put on traditional clothing for festivals and national holidays.

Greek men's traditional clothing is white and red. They might wear a loose-fitting, white cotton shirt. A white double skirt similar to a kilt also is part of men's traditional clothing. They wear a cloth belt and cotton pants under the skirt. A red woolen vest and a red fez complete the outfit. In some parts of Greece, men prefer loose-fitting pants with a jacket or vest.

Greek women's traditional clothing often is in layers. Women might wear a cotton underdress or pants topped with another colorful dress, a vest, or jacket. They often wear an apron over the dress. Many Greek women also wear scarves on their heads.

Traditional Greek clothing includes a skirt and red fez.

Sports and Games

Greeks started the Olympic Games in 776 B.C. The ancient Olympic Games were held in the city of Olympia every four years. The athletes competed in events such as foot races, wrestling, and long jumping. Winners were crowned with a wreath made of olive vines.

Athletes attended the Games even during a war. Everyone agreed to stop fighting during the five days of the Olympic Games.

The Games ended in A.D. 393. They started again in 1896. Now, Winter and Summer Olympic Games are held every four years. Athens will host the 2004 Summer Olympics.

Greeks play all kinds of sports. Soccer is the national sport. Weight lifting and basketball also are popular.

Greeks also enjoy dancing. They dance at family reunions and national celebrations.

Basketball is a popular sport in Greece.

Holidays and Celebrations

The most important holiday in Greece is Easter. On Easter, people celebrate the day Jesus rose from the dead. About 98 percent of the people in Greece are Greek Orthodox Christians. Christianity follows the teachings of Jesus Christ.

The 40 days before Easter is a time of fasting called Lent. People often give up eating meat, eggs, fish, or milk products during Lent.

Most people go to Easter church service. After the service, families get together for a big meal. They usually eat roast lamb. A kind of sweet, braided bread called tsoureki (tsoo-REH-kee) is a popular holiday dish.

March 25 is Greek Independence Day. Greeks hold parades to celebrate the day the Greek War of Independence started in 1821. Turkey had ruled Greece since 1453. The Greeks fought to become a free, independent country.

Greeks celebrate Independence Day with folk dancing.

Hands On: An Egg-Cracking Contest

Greek children have egg-cracking contests at Easter.

What You Need

An adult to help
Saucepan
Water
One egg for each child
Stove
Timer
Dye

What You Do

1. Fill the saucepan about two-thirds full with water. Place the eggs in the water.
2. Ask an adult to help you with the stove.
3. Heat the water until it begins to boil. Set the timer for 10 minutes to make hard-boiled eggs.
4. Remove the saucepan from heat. Let the eggs cool. Remove them from the pan.
5. Follow the instructions on the package of dye. Dye the eggs. Allow the eggs to dry.
6. Everyone gets one egg. Tap your egg against someone else's egg. One egg will crack.
7. The child with the last uncracked egg is the winner.

Learn to Speak Greek

The Greek language has existed for more than 3,000 years. Greek letters are different from the letters in English. There are 24 letters in the Greek alphabet.

hello	γεια σου	(ya-SOO)
good-bye	αντιο	(ahn-DEE-oh)
yes	ναι	(NE)
no	οχι	(OH-kee)
thank you	ευχαριστω	(ef-har-ISS-toh)

Words to Know

ancient (AYN-shunt)—very old

democracy (di-MOK-ruh-see)—a system of government in which citizens vote for their leaders in elections

fasting (FAST-ing)—giving up eating for a time

fez (FEZ)—a round, red felt cap with no brim

peninsula (puh-NIN-suh-luh)—land surrounded by water on three sides

ruins (ROO-inz)—the remains of a building that has been destroyed

traditional (truh-DISH-uh-nuhl)—using the styles, manners, and ways of the past

Read More

Adare, Sierra. *Greece: The People.* The Lands, Peoples, and Cultures Series. New York: Crabtree Publishing, 1999.

Yeoh, Hong Nam. *Greece.* Countries of the World. Milwaukee: Gareth Stevens, 1999.

Useful Addresses and Internet Sites

Embassy of Greece
2211 Massachusetts Avenue NW
Washington, DC 20008

Embassy of the Hellenic Republic
76-80 MacLaren Street
Ottawa, ON K2P 0K6
Canada

ePlay—Explore Greece
http://www.eplay.com/1999-01-09/etravel/cow.adp
The World Factbook 1999—Greece
http://www.odci.gov/cia/publications/factbook/gr.html

Index